GILLIAN CLEMENTS was born and brought up in Sussex, and studied Illustration under Raymond Briggs at Brighton Polytechnic. She has a fascination for world history and a passion for architecture. Gillian's first book for Frances Lincoln was *The Picture History of Great Inventors* which was followed by *The Picture History of Great Explorers.* She lives in Hereford, England.

For P.

With thanks to Derek John and all those at Frances Lincoln
who helped and advised me as I worked on this book.

The Publishers would like to thank Derek John ARIBA
for acting as the consultant for this book.

The Picture History of Great Buildings copyright © Frances Lincoln Limited 2007
Text and illustrations copyright © Gillian Clements 2007

First published in Great Britain in 2007 and in the USA in 2008 by
Frances Lincoln Children's Books, 4 Torriano Mews,
Torriano Avenue, London NW5 2RZ

www.franceslincoln.com

First paperback published in Great Britain in 2011

A catalogue record for this book is available from the British Library.

ISBN: 978-1-84780-036-7

The illustrations for this book are watercolour.

Printed in Dongguan, Guangdong, China by South China Printing in April 2011.

1 3 5 7 9 8 6 4 2

THE PICTURE HISTORY OF
GREAT BUILDINGS

GILLIAN CLEMENTS

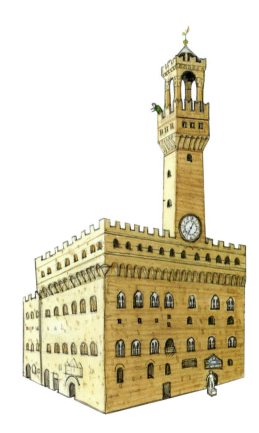

FRANCES LINCOLN
CHILDREN'S BOOKS

Contents

Long ago, people built their homes and shelters out of natural materials. There were no great buildings, just a roof over the head – protection from weather and a harsh environment.

Centuries passed. Most hunter-gatherers abandoned their nomadic lifestyles to build houses, and in time, towns. Cities grew. Men who had acquired exceptional building skills began designing great monuments, like the ziggurats of the Fertile Crescent (now Iraq), and the pyramids of Ancient Egypt.

Throughout history, religion and culture have often been the driving forces behind architects' and engineers' greatest buildings. From the 19th century, technology and new materials have given architects the ability to design breathtaking buildings – structures that even reach to the sky.

But what of the future? Perhaps now is the time to build 'green' homes and workplaces that work in harmony with our fragile climate.

In the meantime, I hope this book tells the entertaining story of some of our world's greatest Great Buildings.

Gillian Clements

THE FIRST HOMES

In prehistoric times, people used whatever they could find to make shelters for themselves against the weather. They made these homes from wood, stone, mud, reeds and even animal skins and bones. If they were lucky they lived in caves.

People first built simple shelters about 12,000 years ago, changing and perfecting them over many generations. Some people still build homes like this today, following in the footsteps of their ancestors.

Paintings found on the walls of caves in southern France are believed to be 20,000 years old.

Huts in Mesopotamia were made from

marshland reeds which kept them cool in the warm weather.

Mud from rivers (sun-dried or fired to make bricks) was an ideal building material. A protective skin of fired bricks, plaster or limewash covered important buildings.

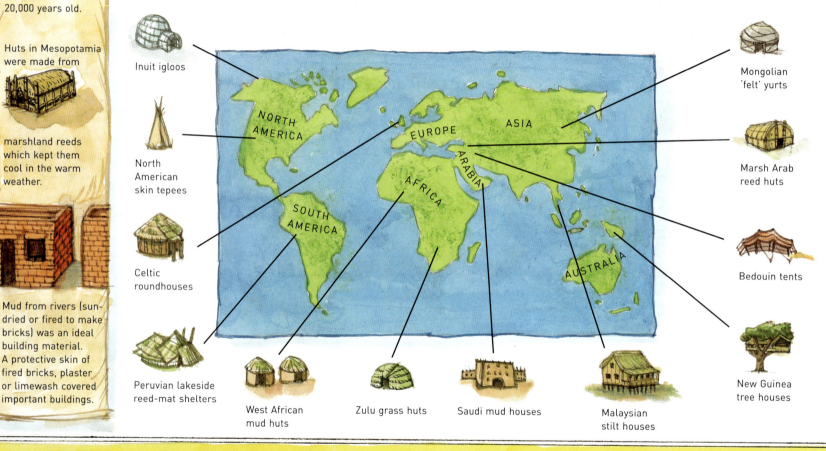

Inuit igloos

North American skin tepees

Celtic roundhouses

Peruvian lakeside reed-mat shelters

West African mud huts

Zulu grass huts

Saudi mud houses

Malaysian stilt houses

Mongolian 'felt' yurts

Marsh Arab reed huts

Bedouin tents

New Guinea tree houses

The first buildings were simple shelters made from natural materials.

1 million years ago Neanderthal people make clothes from skins and live in caves.

100,000–35,000 years ago Modern humans survive the Ice Age by living in caves and hunting.

8300 BC After the great Ice Age, there are new continents. Farming begins to develop.

Jericho

8000 BC Jericho, near the Dead Sea, is one of the earliest villages.

6000 BC People use a wheel to make pottery and copper instead of stone to make strong tools.

THE FIRST CITIES
From 5000 BC

Where the climate was good and the land fertile, people chose to become farmers. They grew food instead of hunting for it. With more than enough to eat inside the new farming settlements, some villagers were free to learn crafts or to build homes, and the first cities of the world began to take shape. The growth of the world's first cities is called the Urban Revolution, and it was most widespread in the Nile delta and between the rivers Tigris and Euphrates around 5,000 years ago. Many thousands of people started living together in new class systems, with ruling families in charge at the top, and workers and slaves at the bottom.

The first cities usually had strong stone walls protecting the homes inside. The gates of the city were guarded by soldiers and were locked at night or if the city was under attack. Market stalls were set up at the gateways to attract buyers going through the city gates.

Safe inside the walls, the people started to develop writing, science, and astronomy – and built great temples and palaces.

Jerico's stone walls were built over 9,000 years ago, enclosing a town of around 2,000 people. This clay-covered skull was found at the ancient site.

The ancient city of Catal Huyuk in today's Turkey is around 8,000 years old, and it was occupied for many centuries.

Amongst the houses, this fresco of hunters surrounding a great red bull must have adorned a special religious place.

The Assyrian city of **Korsabad** (742-706 BC) had temples and palaces built within its strong walls.

Most urban societies divided themselves into separate classes.

Ruling families

Priests

Nobles

Important citizens

Merchants and Craftsmen

Workers and slaves

The great city of Jericho was one of the world's earliest cities, although many of the great ancient cities grew up in river valleys. Jericho's thick stone walls date back thousands of years to the Neolithic Age, when people began to settle and farm. Nearby water was vital to their survival.

Most of the world's first great cities developed in fertile river valleys.

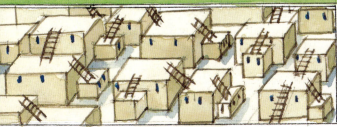

c. 6000 BC The ancient city of Catal Huyuk was built of mud-bricks. The flat-roofed houses were so close together that the only way to travel about was across the rooftops!

5000 BC Egyptian and Mesopotamian farmers use river water to irrigate their fields.

3000 BC Cities appear independently in different parts of the world, beginning in the Middle East at Ur, Uruk, Babylon and Nineveh.

ANCIENT MONUMENTS

The Sumerians and the Egyptians were the first to build great monumental buildings but many ancient civilisations followed their example. Made of brick or stone, these were buildings meant to last, and to demonstrate the power of their gods and kings.

GREAT BRITAIN

Carnac

FRANCE

ITALY

Rome

SPAIN

GREECE

CRETE

Mediterranean sea

PAGAN EUROPE

Circles and lines of standing stones were ingeniously raised on sites across western Europe, from Sweden to Malta and also in the British Isles. The stones' purpose is a mystery but their siting was the work of Stone Age people, organised into huge teams, who dragged the massive stones long distances across the landscape and set them upright.

① **Stonehenge** grew in size over many centuries, into an impressive stone circle. The massive outer sandstone blocks weighed about 40 tonnes, and the inner blue stones were dragged 240 kilometres (150 miles) from Preselly in Wales to Salisbury Plain.

THE ROMANS

The Romans ruled Italy from around 265 BC, and also conquered North Africa, around the Mediterranean and southern Europe and into Asia Minor. Roman public buildings were copied throughout the Empire under emperors from Augustus (31 BC) onward, and their grid-designed cities were built in stone, brick, volcanic rock (tufa, pumice and lava), terracotta and concrete. Concrete was a great invention, allowing Romans to develop arches, vaults and domes.

② **Hadrian's Wall** was built in about 122 AD, at the height of the Roman Empire. The Emperor Hadrian ordered the great stone wall to be built in Britannia, at the edge of his empire. Acting as a defence and as a frontier trading control, it lay between Roman-occupied land and Scotland to the north.

ANCIENT GREECE & CRETE

Ancient Crete (c. 2000-1450 BC), with its Minoan palaces and mythical Minotaur, was an early manifestation of the civilisation of Ancient Greece. Later, in around 1250 BC, on the mainland of Mycenae, the Greek civilisation built palaces and royal tombs. Around 500 BC, great city-states like Athens built magnificent temples and theatres.

③ **The Tomb of Agammemnon/the Treasury of Atreus** at Mycenae was a beehive-shaped 13-metre-high (43 feet) chamber, built underground but open to the sky, with a corridor access cut into the hillside.

Monumental buildings of the ancient world were built to last forever.

4700 BC Western Europeans begin to erect stone religious monuments like at Carnac in Brittany (France).

c. 3200 BC The White Temple, Uruk is built of stone, brick & tile. Protective limewash gives it its name.

3200 – 2400 BC Simple brick or stone tombs (mastabas) are first built at Memphis, Egypt's capital and centre of government in its Old Kingdom.

ASSYRIA (c. 1100–600 BC)

The borders of this empire reached from the Persian Gulf to the Mediterranean, and up to the Black Sea. The fierce Assyrians lived in northern Mesopotamia by the River Tigris, but their army defeated strong Syrian, Babylonian, Egyptian, Judean and Phoenician forces to create the largest empire of its day.

④

The ziggurat temple at Ashur

(c. 1250 BC) Between 3000–500 BC, all the great Mesopotamian city-states built brick ziggurats. The Assyrians built 3 at their capital, Ashur. The walls were very thick to compensate for the weak mud bricks, and the builders also added whitewash or patterned, coloured cones to further protect the temples.

MESOPOTAMIA

Sumerians built stepped pyramids called ziggurats in cities like Uruk, on man-made, stepped mounds. The temple stood at the top. Sargon the Great of Akkad conquered the Sumerians in c. 2800 BC.

⑤

The Pillar Temple, Uruk

(c. 3000–2500 BC) had free-standing, coloured palm tree-style pillars. The temple was decorated with coloured mud cone mosaics and could be seen from great distances. It symbolised the bridge between the gods and people.

BABYLON

Lying for 2,000 years on the banks of the River Euphrates, Babylon (c. 600 BC) was at the centre of a great empire. King Nebuchadnezzar fortified Babylon and created gardens to make it one of the most beautiful Mesopotamian cities, and a centre for trade and learning.

⑥

Tower of Babel

This 7-storey spiral ziggurat of Etemenanki was faced with blue-glazed bricks, and rose from a 90 metre (295 feet) square base.

Black Sea

Caspian Sea

River Tigris

River Euphrates

④

⑤ ⑥

⑦

⑧

Persian Gulf

EGYPT

PERSIA

The Persian Empire finally included Babylon, Anatolia, Palestine, and even parts of Egypt and India. Darius the 1st built a palace at Persepolis in a distinctive Persian style, using craftsmen from Assyria, Egypt and Greece, and Babylonian brick-makers.

⑦

Persepolis's **Hall of a Hundred Columns** (begun c. 518 BC) used glazed, coloured bricks. The painted wooded ceiling was held up by a forest of columns.

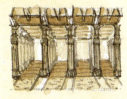

EGYPT

Menes, the first known Egyptian king, united the Upper and Lower Egyptian kingdoms in c. 3200 BC. People believed the Pharaohs were gods as well as kings and the buildings that housed their bodies symbolised their royal power in the Afterlife.

⑧

The 3 pyramids and the sphinx at Giza

(c. 2500 BC). The Great Pyramid was 146 metres (480 feet) high. The burial chamber was 70 metres (230 feet) above ground in the exact centre of the pyramid. The granite sarcophagus had been dragged into the granite-lined chamber.

They represented the power of the civilisation's gods and kings.

c. 1500–1100 BC Mycenaeans build fortifications in Greece.

c. 600 BC King Nebuchadnezzar orders the building of Babylon's Hanging Gardens.

c. 500–300 BC A great palace is begun by Daruis the Great at Persepolis, the new capital of his Persian Empire.

Imhotep

Pharaoh Djoser

THE STEP PYRAMID
Saqqara, Egypt, c. 2680 BC

This was the first great stone building in the world. Built at Saqqara on the banks of the River Nile, it stood a gigantic 60 metres (196 feet) high! The Pyramid's creator was Imhotep, the first architect we know of in history. It was built for Pharaoh Djoser. Deep underground, below the impressive pyramid, Imhotep planned the dead Pharaoh's real burial chamber. It was hidden to protect his mummified body and possessions he would need in the Afterlife. The ancient Egyptians did not want tomb robbers to steal what they believed belonged to their king in his eternal life after death. Like the other famous pyramids at nearby Giza, the Step Pyramid was built with astonishing accuracy. After studying the night sky, surveyors carefully aligned its site exactly to the compass points of north, south, east and west.

Imhotep's stepped pyramid was built of stone to last for 'eternity', and was much stronger than earlier mud-brick mastaba tombs.

Work masters organised many thousands of labourers into work gangs. These gangs hacked the limestone blocks out of solid rock using copper chisels and dragged the heavy blocks up ramps. Skilled craftsmen shaped the stone and made sure each layer was set perfectly level. Their tools were incredibly accurate, leaving just tiny joints to be filled with mortar.

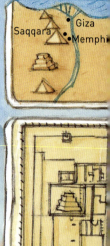

Imhotep's pyramid was the main feature in a huge network of temples and tombs, built to house the remains and belongings of royal family members. The whole area was a place for rituals of death.

It took many years of skilful organisation to plan, find labour, then build the pyramid.

3000–2500 BC The 900-towered great wall of Uruk is built.

c. 2500 BC Using simple ropes and levers, workers drag rock-laden sledges higher and higher up ramps to complete the pyramids.

2100–1500 BC On the island of Crete, the Minoans build a famous palace at Knossos.

1250 BC The new temple at Karnak in Egypt is dedicated to the god Amun.

Iktinos and Kallikrates

THE PARTHENON
Athens, Greece, 447–38 BC

GREECE

Athens

The architects used visual tricks on the temple. Columns that bulged outwards slightly, actually looked straight. Although they looked equally spaced, the columns were spaced unevenly and leaned inwards. Even the plinth bulged upwards to make it appear flat.

The Parthenon was just a part of the sacred site called the Akropolis. Processions approached by walking up a steep, easily-defended hill and through an entrance gate. Inside were temples and statues.

Labourers and oxen had to haul everything up to the Akropolis. Men shifted stones into place using simple ramps and cranes but gravity and metal clamps held most of the stonework together.

This impressive marble temple took just 9 years to build. Perikles, a famous statesman from Athens, commissioned it and dedicated it to the goddess Athena – the Greek goddess of wisdom. The temple was a place to meet and worship – a typical Greek temple of columns, lintels, and massive roof timbers. But the Parthenon's beautiful design and magnificent position is what makes it special. The architects worked out every proportion in tiny detail to make the finished temple appear perfect. There are 8 columns at each end of the Parthenon, and 17 along the sides. All of them rest on a 3-step plinth which provides a level base on the rocky outcrop. Originally, Athena's temple was very colourful and full of sculpture. There was a huge gold and ivory statue of Athena inside, and rich decoration on the frieze and pediments.

Today, the Parthenon is a ruin as it was used for storing gunpowder in the 18th century and an explosion blew off the roof. Many of the sculptures located in the frieze were broken up and sold to a British diplomat called Lord Elgin. They can be seen at the British Museum in London.

The Greeks devised certain styles of capitals for the temple columns, and for all other vertical shapes on the temple.

Doric capitals
The simplest of the styles, the capital (top of the column) is carved from a single stone block.

Ionic capitals
A style originating on the Ionian coast, the Ionic capital is more decorative than the Doric.

Corinthian capitals
Based on the Ionic style, the Corinthian capital also has a stylised acanthus leaf decoration.

Athens, a rich city-state, built a 'perfect' marble temple on the summit of the rocky Akropolis.

c. 600 BC In the city of Babylon, King Nebuchadnezzar builds the magnificent Ishtar Gate using blue-glazed bricks.

300 BC Dinocrates and Greek engineers build the Egyptian city of Alexandria, and a great lighthouse on the island of Pharos at the mouth of the Nile.

c. 210 BC Emperor Qin Shi Huang Ti rules a newly-unified China, and builds the 6,000 kilometre (3,730 mile) long Great Wall along China's northern boundary, to protect them from invading Huns.

Because the iron frame of the new industrial buildings carried the whole weight of the roof, the walls no longer had to be load-bearing. They could be delicate and thin. Architects also designed railway stations, some in classical styles with beautiful glass and iron train sheds.

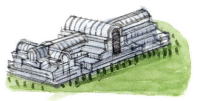

Galleria Vittorio Emanuele the 2nd
Milan, 1829/1865–67
Giuseppe Mengoni (1829–77)
This beautiful pedestrian street has iron and glass vaults and a dome over 19th century Milanese buildings.

Crystal Palace, London Exhibition, 1851
Joseph Paxton (1801–65)
This massive glass and steel structure was 564 metres (1,850 feet) long, and used 300,000 plate glass sheets – none longer than 125 centimetres (49 inches). Yet it only took 2,000 men 3 months to build.

Gare de l'Est Paris, 1847–52
François-Alexrandre Duquesney
Duquesney (1790–1849) built this Renaissance-style railway station. Its iron and glass shed had a span of over 30 metres (100 feet)!

Paddington Station London, 1852,
I.K. Brunel (see page 42)
Railway stations were called the 'Cathedrals' of the Age. Brunel's shed had three wrought-iron framed spans, which were intersected by cross vaults.

Sir Henry Bessemer (1813–98) proved important for the Industrial Age because of his new steel-making process. His steel was less brittle than cast iron and less bendable than wrought iron. Bessemer's steel, and the newly-invented 'plate glass' were used together in many new stations, arcades and palm houses.

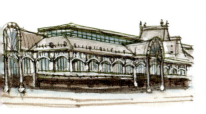

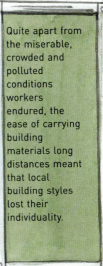

Les Halles Centrales
Paris, begun 1853
Victor Baltard (1805–74)
This fruit and vegetable market had connected iron sheds roofed with glass and iron, and were spacious and light.

Oriel Chambers Liverpool, 1864
Peter Ellis (c. 1835–84)
This 5-storey office building had a cast-iron frame, but used it in a very ornate way.

Magazins du Bon Marche
Paris, 1876, Gustave Eiffel (see page 45) & Louis-Charles Boileau (1812–96)
The huge space in this shopping arcade was lit naturally through a glass and iron roof. There were several shopping levels, cross-linked with bridges.

Galerie des Machines,
Paris Exhibition, 1889, Charles Dutert (1845–1906) with engineer Victor Contamin (1840–93)
This ambitious glass and steel exhibition space was huge – 430 by 120 metres (1,410 by 393 feet) and 45 metres (148 feet) high. It was the greatest span then built and looked like a huge bridge arch.

Quite apart from the miserable, crowded and polluted conditions workers endured, the ease of carrying building materials long distances meant that local building styles lost their individuality.

Victorian glass and steel structures paved the way for skyscraper buildings.

1858 G.T. Greene designs an architecturally advanced iron-framed boat store at the Sheerness navy dockyard.

1859–67 Like the earlier Bibliotèque St Genevieve (pictured), Labrouste's Bibliothèque Nationale has a beautiful, delicately-designed cast-iron frame.

John Roebling *(1806-69)*

Washington Roeb... *(1837-1926)*

BROOKLYN BRIDGE
New York, USA, 1867–83

John Roebling was born in Germany. He began the bridge in 1867 but in 1869 his foot was crushed between a ferry and the quay while overseeing the building work. John died three weeks later from tetanus. His son, Washington Roebling, took over from his father but was eventually taken from the site suffering from 'the bends', a terrible illness caused by nitrogen bubbles forming in the blood of divers. Many workers got this while labouring in caissons under the East River. This illness nearly killed him. Washington's wife, Emily, finally finished the bridge under his instructions.

wire trusses

suspension cable

Brooklyn Bridge spanned the East River, joining the cities of Manhattan and Brooklyn. Horse-drawn carriages used the two outer lanes. Cable cars travelled or the inside lanes, and pedestrians crossed on a central elevated walkway.

The spectacular Brooklyn Bridge, built over New York's East River, was a triumph of new engineering and new architecture. Its engineer, John Roebling, used super-modern steel suspension cables on his bridge – and he designed the masonry piers, sunk into the river-bed, in an imaginative mixture of ancient Egyptian, Roman and Gothic styles. Egypt symbolised strength, Rome represented civic greatness, and the Gothic reflected elegance. The bridge took 16 years to build because they had to build the piers below the river-bed. During constuction, over 20 workers lost their lives.

John Roebling hung his bridge's roadbed from the steel suspension cables, using thinner vertical wire. And, to make the bridge even stronger, he had diagonal wires stretched from the granite towers and along the roadway.

A double system of steel suspension cables held the enormous weight of Brooklyn Bridge's roadbed.

1846 Robert Stephenson's High Level railway bridge over the River Tyne, is one of the last cast-iron bridges.

1882–89 Sir Benjamin Baker builds the magnificent Forth Bridge in Scotland.

1884 Eiffel designs the 165-metre-long (541 feet) ironwork span for the Garabit Viaduct.

EIFFEL TOWER
Paris, France, 1887–89

Alexandre Gustave Eiffel
(1832–1923)

The Eiffel Tower still dominates Paris two centuries on – it is the city's most popular tourist destination. But it was not always so. In Eiffel's day most Parisians hated it, saying the tower ruined the city's skyline. And they said it was an insult to the cathedral and palaces that it dwarfed.

Paris hosted its own Great Exposition in 1889, and the most eye-catching exhibit was the amazing, modern, 300-metre-high (984 feet) Eiffel Tower. The simple all-metal structure was the tallest in the world, and demonstrated how advanced French skills were in this kind of engineering. Eiffel's intention to impress the world succeeded.

By June 1887 the builders had finished preparing the tower's deep foundations. Then, using cranes and wooden scaffolding, they began construction on the tower's four legs, just as if they were bridge arches. Above the arches, the tower's tapering criss-cross metalwork design was there for strength and decoration. Each of the 12,000 iron pieces was prefabricated, then quickly and accurately riveted together on site. Everything was finished by April 1889, ready for the Exposition. The tower was strong and stable enough to withstand the very worst gales.

It took two and a half million rivets to hold the Eiffel Tower together. Because Parisians worried that the Tower might fall, extra ironwork was built in to convince them of its strength. This ironwork is only decoration – it isn't really needed.

Eiffel built the hidden steel skeleton or armature inside Bartholdi's Statue of Liberty sculpture. It gives New York's 91-metre-high (300 feet) landmark the strength to stand up.

At Paris' 1889 exposition, the Eiffel Tower and the Galerie des Machines were the greatest engineering exhibits.

1880 At long last, after 532 years, Cologne Cathedral is finished.

NEW YORK'S FIRST SKYSCRAPERS
Late 19th to early 20th centuries

By the late 1800s, architects had devised a new way of building New York's big department stores, offices and factories. Recent inventions and factory mass-production had made exciting new skyscrapers possible, aided by a plentiful supply of money and solid ground. This vertical building style was perfect for a city like New York troubled by scarce and expensive land. The new multi-storey buildings had masonry walls hanging from rigid steel frames. As its buildings rose higher and higher, New York became a famous Skyscraper City.

Art Deco was a style of decoration in the 1920s and 30s that featured geometric shapes and bold colours. Examples can be found in many buildings of the time.

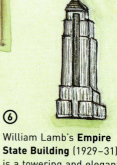

⑥ William Lamb's **Empire State Building** (1929-31) is a towering and elegant Art Deco skyscraper. During construction its steel frame was bolted and riveted together, then concrete was poured on to it. Next they fitted the windows and limestone cladding before laying the bricks. Finally the lifts were installed.

⑤ Cass Gilbert's **Woolworth Building** (1910-13) is 241 metres (791 feet) high. This popular skyscraper had terracotta cladding and Gothic decoration over a steel frame. At 60 storeys it needed huge foundations at least 17 metres (56 feet) deep.

① J.P. Gaynor's **Haughwout Store** (1856) was built in a 16th century Venetian style, but using prefabricated cast-iron sections bolted together – including its store front. In 1857 it had the first passenger lift in any town building.

② Richard M. Hunt's **Tribune Building** (1870s) was a very plain, undecorated building, 9 storeys and 80 metres (262 feet) high. It was one of the first true skyscrapers.

③ George B. Post's **Western Union Telegraph Building** (1873-75) is 10 storeys and 70 metres (230 feet) high.

④ The **Park Row Building** (1899), with 36 storeys, was the world's highest building when it was constructed.

Early skyscapers hid their steel frames under heavy, decorated masonry.

1871 A huge fire destroys thousands of timber-framed buildings in Chicago.

1873-86 The Great Western Railway Company builds a tunnel between England and Wales under England's River Severn estuary.

1879-84 Alexandre Gustave Eiffel builds the steel skeleton that holds up New York's Statue of Liberty.

1881 George B. Post builds New York's Produce Exchange.

CHICAGO'S FIRST SKYSCRAPERS
Late 19th to early 20th centuries

The work of the Chicago School of Architects (c.1850) looked to the future. There were three teams – Burnham and Root, Holabird and Roche and Adler and Sullivan. The older William Le Baron Jenney, and the imaginative Frank Lloyd Wright, were also very important Chicago architects.

The **Arts and Crafts** Movement reacted against buildings of the Machine Age. They believed that craftsmen should use local materials – definitely not metal frames – to create buildings untouched by modern industrial ways.

Many of Chicago's buildings were timber-framed before the terrible fire of 1871, which wiped out much of the city. The awful destruction gave architects the chance to build a modern Chicago in steel. When the building boom made land expensive, they took advantage of new building materials, and up-to-the-minute inventions, to build upwards. Chicago became a skyscraper city, like New York.

① William Le Baron Jenney's **Home Insurance Building** (1884–85) had floors that were supported by the building's iron and steel frame. However, Jenney thought that the building's brick walls needed to support themselves – and so he built them thickly. Despite this, it was the first true skyscraper because of its strong, riveted, fire-proof steel frame.

② William Holarbird and Martin Roche's **Tacoma Building** (1887–89) had a steel frame that supported its floors and walls – another true skyscraper.

③ Dankmar Adler and Louis Sullivan's **Walker Warehouse** (1888–89) was a very modern-style building, though its masonry façade had a Classical look.

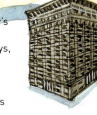

⑥ Burnham and Company's **Reliance Building** (1894–95) had 13 storeys, with very light curtain-wall cladding over its steel skeleton. The building's top 10 storeys were built in only 15 days!

⑤ Holarbird and Roche's **Marquette Building** (1893–94) was a typical strong-looking Chicago building, built in a Classical style.

④ D.H. Burnham and J.W. Root's **Monadnock Building** (1891) was the last tall iron-framed building, at 7 storeys high, that had thick, load-bearing masonry walls.

The first true skyscrapers, in Chicago, hung their thin walls from rigid steel frames.

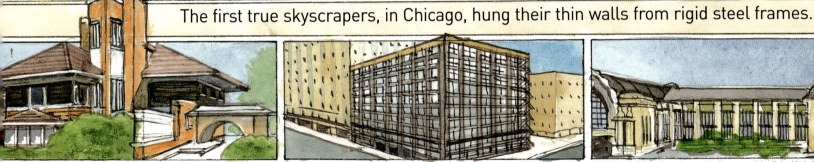

1893 In Illinois, Frank Lloyd Wright builds his new-style Winslow House.

1904 Holabird and Roche's West Jackson Boulevard Building rises in 20th-century Chicago.

1904-14 Eliel Saarinen designs and builds Helsinki's Central Railway Station using clear, simple shapes and lines.

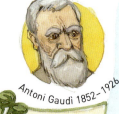

Antoni Gaudì 1852–1926

The **Art Nouveau** style of decoration became popular at the end of the 19th century, especially for interiors, illustrations and jewellery.

In Paris, Hector Guimard (1867–1942) used the Art Nouveau style to design the curvy, plant-like cast-iron and wrought-iron entrances to the Métro.

SAGRADA FAMILIA
Barcelona, Spain, begun 1882

The Catalan architect, Antoni Gaudì, spent most of his later career working on just one project – the Sagrada Familia in Barcelona, Spain. Gaudì was very religious, and, inspired by God and Nature, this cathedral-like temple was his most precious work.

But still, a hundred years after building began, it remains unfinished. The Sagrada Familia is an extraordinary building, looking more like a growing, living thing than a building. Gaudì chose to create it in the Art Nouveau style he had already used in buildings like the Casa Batllo (the strange and animal-like building known as the House of Bones). Art Nouveau was an especially popular style in Barcelona, his beloved home city.

Over the Sagrada Familia's 100-metre-long (328 feet) nave rises a group of towers – the largest representing Christ. The four towers over the temple's western façade represent the 12 apostles.

The building shows off its colour, curves and rounded, organic shapes. Gaudì even made the tall, thin columns supporting the vaults inside, lean inwards – which makes them look like a stone forest.

Art Nouveau architecture was rarer than its art. But Gaudì designed the curvaceous-style homes at Park Güell (1900–14), the Casa Mila (1905–10) and Casa Batllo (1905–7) buildings

Barcelona Catalans like Gaudì loved Art Nouveau's flowery, flowing style.

1892–93 Victor Horta's Hotel Tassel, Brussels, is decorated with swirling paintings and mosaic designs.

1898–99 Otto Wagner creates an Art Nouveau façade for his Majolica House in Vienna.

1909 C.R. Mackintosh, the Scottish architect and designer, completes his Glasgow School of Art.

1920–21 Erich Mendelsohn builds the Art Nouveau-style Einstein Tower near Potsdam, Germany.

Walter Gropius (1883–1969)

THE BAUHAUS
Germany, 1919–33

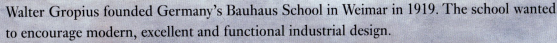

Walter Gropius founded Germany's Bauhaus School in Weimar in 1919. The school wanted to encourage modern, excellent and functional industrial design.

Relocating to Dessau in 1925, the 3-block Bauhaus Building contained workshops, classrooms and a 5-storey tower of studios and dormitories. Plain glass walls in the Bauhaus's workshops, and solid walled classrooms demonstrated the school's functional design.

When Hitler and his Nazi Party came to power in Germany, they detested the politics of the Bauhaus's brilliant, free-thinking students and teachers. They closed the school in 1933, and many of these exceptional people emigrated to America and became important architects there.

In 1908, Peter Behrens (1868–1940) designed the Classical-looking **AEG Turbine Factory** in Berlin. Some of Behrens's design assistants such as Gropius, Le Corbusier, and Mies van der Rohe were to become famous architects themselves.

The Fagus Factory (1911–13)
Walter Gropius and Adolf Meyer designed the Fagus Factory at Alfeld-an-der-Leine in Germany, and began a fashionable functional style for factories all around the world.

Italian Futurists
In 1914, two young architects, Antonio Sant'Elia and Mario Chiattone, made amazing futurist designs of a new city, **Citta Nuova**. Inspired by science and technology, the futurists wanted buildings to be light and practical. Nothing was built, but the two men's drawings and designs remain.

Dutch De Stijl artists (from 1917) wanted art and architecture to be central to people's lives. Aiming to design good Modern post-war housing – just as the Bauhaus did in Germany – they built several mass-housing schemes in Holland.

The Bauhaus designed modern functional buildings made of glass and steel.

1924 Gerrit Thomas Rietveld's famous Schroeder House is built in Utrecht, Holland.

1926–30 Karl Ehn's 'wall' of houses – the Karl-Marx-Hof in Vienna – contains flats, offices and many local services.

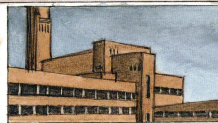
1926 Willem Marinus Dudok builds a modern town hall in Hilversum, Holland.

1930 J.F. Staal's multi-storey block of housing, the De Wlkenkrabbe is completed in Amsterdam, Holland.

William van Alen (1883–1954)

THE CHRYSLER BUILDING
New York, USA, 1928–30

The complete view of the Chrysler Building.

Land prices continued to rise in 1920s New York. So did its skyscrapers – especially in the financial area around Wall Street.

The Chrysler Building was in East 42nd Street and for just one year, the 319-metre-high (1,047 feet), 77-storey grey and white brick skyscraper was the highest in the world. Cleverly, the architect William van Alen hid the skyscraper's 56 metre (184 feet) spire in its unfinished elevator shaft until the very last moment. Once in place, the Chrysler Building became 37 metres (121 feet) higher than New York's Bank of Manhattan!

Like many rival New York architects, van Alen had wanted to make his skyscraper a towering, modern and exciting building – just the right sort of headquarters for an ambitious car magnate like Walter Chrysler. Van Alen had chosen to decorate the building, inside and out, in the popular Art Deco style. In fact, the Chrysler Building became instantly famous for the triangular silver sunburst design on the stainless steel curves of its spire, and the metal eagles watching high over the New York streets.

Russian skyscrapers
In 1933, Boris Iofan won the competition for Moscow's new 'Palace of the Soviets', designed as a 415 metre (1,365 feet) high building for government, educational and leisure use, topped with a 100-metre (325 feet) high statue of Lenin! But World War II arrived, so it was never built.

In the race to be the highest, the Chrysler Building was overtaken by the Empire State Building.

1903–13 New York's magnificent French-style Grand Central Station is designed.

1927–29 Konstantin Melnikov builds Rusakov Worker's Club in Moscow in the constructivist style.

1930 Raymond M. Hood's futurist-looking Daily News Building in New York is totally unornamented.

1931–39 The Rockefeller Centre in New York groups city buildings and facilities around open spaces instead of using a single skyscraper.

UNITÉ D'HABITATION

Marseille, France, 1946–52

Le Corbusier (1887–1965)

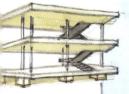

1914 Domino House flexible construction

Machines for Living In
Le Corbusier wanted houses to work well – to be functional – and beautiful. He didn't intend that homes should actually be impersonal machines.

side view of the Unité d'Habitation

Le Corbusier, a Swiss whose real name was Charles-Eduoard Jeanneret, was a modern Renaissance Man and one of the most important architects of the 20th century. He was an artist, thinker and craftsman, as well as an architect of the Machine Age. Searching for ideas Le Corbusier toured Europe before settling in France and, in 1923, writing *Vers une Architecture* – a book outlining his views. He believed that modern architects should welcome a new industrial spirit. Buildings, he said, should be 'machines for living in'. This idea influenced architects all over the world. Le Corbusier's own Unité d'Habitation in Marseilles – a neighbourhood-in-a-block – was intended to live up to his beliefs.

It was a bold rectangular shape – a huge, modern, concrete, glass and steel housing-block lifted up on stilts called piloti. L'Unité held more than 300 apartments of varying sizes, and its 1,600 residents had all the facilities of a small town on their doorstep and rooftop.

With attention to detail, Corbusier created a shopping street within the building, sports facilities, and double-height living rooms – all intended to make the residents' lives as easy as possible.

Villa Savoye
Corbusier invented a system of proportions, just as architects in Classical Greece and Renaissance Italy had done. He wanted a home's proportions to be comfortable to live in, and look beautiful – like his white Villa Savoye, Poissy (1929–30)

In his Unité D'Habitation, Corbusier worked out how to house an entire community.

1946 Buckminster-Fuller designs the 'Wichita House' using aircraft assembly-line building techniques – an idea leading to his later Geodesic Domes.

1950–54 Le Corbusier designs a beautiful pilgrimage church, Notre-Dame-du-Haut, at Ronchamp, France.

1965 onwards Walter Segal perfects his ideas on cheap, easily constructed Self-Build homes.

Frank Lloyd Wright
1867-1959

GUGGENHEIM MUSEUM

New York, USA, designed 1943, built 1956-9

The Guggenheim could never have been built without using structural, curved slabs of concrete. Concrete gave architects the freedom to design flowing, curved shapes. They first realised its possibilities in 1905, when Robert Maillart designed a reinforced concrete bridge in Felsegg, Switzerland.

Falling Water (1936-39) Wright's most famous house, built in concrete, was designed to blend in with nature. It had strong horizontal 'cantilevered' balconies that stretched out over the water, and when Wright designed it for millionaire Edgar J. Kaufmann, he told him not to simply look at the waterfalls, but to live with them.

The famous American architect Frank Lloyd Wright began his career in Chicago in the 1890s, building beautiful, spacious homes for the rich. In his long life (he lived to be over 90) he designed many famous and original buildings. Perhaps the most eccentric was one of his last works, New York's Solomon R. Guggenheim Museum. It stands opposite New York's Central Park, like a futuristic spaceship tucked between Fifth Avenue apartment blocks. Wright's idea was to create a simple but unusual shape – a reinforced concrete shell, tapering downwards. Clinging to the shell's inside wall is a spiral walkway that grows wider as it climbs. This is where the museum hangs its paintings. On top of the whole curious structure, Wright put in a glass roof to let plenty of natural light in. Visitors take a lift to the top of the building, then walk slowly down the ramp, admiring the art. There are no pillars, columns or small gallery rooms to spoil their view. There aren't even windows looking out on to the New York streets!

Frank Lloyd Wright used concrete – a strong material capable of taking on interesting shapes.

1909-10 Wright's Robie House in Chicago opens up a new and original house style.

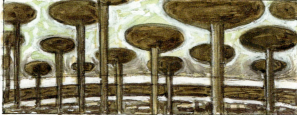

1936-39 Wright builds his Johnson Wax Building, Racine, with a glass roof.

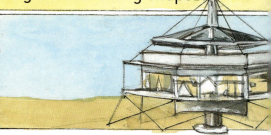

1927 Richard Buckminster-Fuller perfects the prototype for Dymaxion House, an assembled machine for living in.

THE SYDNEY OPERA HOUSE

Sydney, Australia, 1957–73

Jorn Utzon (b. 1918)

So that all of the roof curves looked right together, Utzon made them up as pieces – or segments – of a single sphere.

It is really important that opera houses, concert halls and theatres are built so that the sound travels well inside. At first, Sydney Opera House's shell-shaped roof was very bad acoustically. To help, builders put in plywood and plexiglas surfaces inside the roof.

The Sydney Opera House design competition was won by the Danish architect Jorn Utzon, and looks as dramatic outside as its operas are inside. His design was selected in 1957 but the roof construction was beyond the capabilities of the engineers of that time. It was not until 1961 that the problem with the complex structure was solved. By 1966 there were many cost problems and the government almost stopped construction and Utzon angrily left the project.

Right on Sydney Harbour's waterfront, the building's roof is shaped like sails, or upturned boats, silhouetted against the sky. The engineers made the roof from pre-fabricated concrete ribs, strengthened with steel cables. Then they covered the whole roof with over a million brilliant ceramic tiles – and underneath, for light, put in huge amber-coloured glass windows. A concert hall and the opera theatre itself live in the two largest curving roof shells. The bottom of the building, a huge contrast to the soaring roof, is made of heavy-looking concrete and granite. Utzon built the base on to Sydney's sandstone bedrock at Bennelong Point, where it lies almost surrounded by water.

E qual via scegliete?

Individual architects' designs use new techniques and materials with great imagination.

1967 Richard Buckminster-Fuller's U.S. Pavilion at Expo '67 in Montreal develops his experimental, pre-fabricated dome structure, made of metal or plastic.

1969 Rogers and Piano design the Pompidou Centre, Paris, and bolt the services, such as the escalators, to the outside of the building.

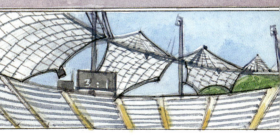

1972 Frei Otto's Olympic Games Tent, Munich, has huge spans and an umbrella roof made of a PVC-coated polyester fabric. It is held up by masts and cables.

WORLD HIGH RISES
1950s onwards

When Mies van der Rohe's Seagram Building was built in New York in 1954, another race began - to build the world's highest skyscraper. This time there was truly world-wide competition - not just American. But why did they build so high? In some cities, like New York, Tokyo and Hong Kong, land is scarce and expensive, and high buildings make sense. Some companies also want prestigious skyscrapers on their own, small, historic sites. But very often, such buildings are the proud boast of architects, clients, cities and even nations, showing off their engineering technology and wealth.

Engineers have had to learn even more sophisticated ways to make the world's vertical cities. Sometimes they design strengthened frames and skins of steel, or they hang the skyscraper's many storeys from a strong central core.

Seagram Building
(New York, 1954, Mies van der Rohe)
Mies was a practical and ambitious architect who left Nazi Germany in the 1930s, and made his name in America. The Seagram Building was his best known skyscraper. It was a practical, functional and beautiful building, making use of the finest brass, marble, bronze, steel and glass.

John Hancock Center,
(Chicago, 1965–70, Skidmore, Owings, Merrill and Khan)
This tapered, 95-storey, 344 metre (1,129 feet) building overtook the Empire State Building as the world's highest. It was not just for corporate offices, people also lived, shopped and stayed there. Khan designed the centre with diagonal outside bracing, for strength against wind and earthquakes.

World Trade Center,
(New York, 1966–73, Minoru Yamasaki)
When these towers were added to the famous New York skyline, they were the world's highest, at 417 metres (1,368 feet). Their strength lay in their clever stressed skin made of steel mesh, unfortunately not strong enough to withstand the terrorist attacks of September 11th 2001.

Sears Tower,
(Chicago, 1974, Fazlur Khan and Bruce Graham)
The 442-metre-high (1,450 feet) Sears Tower was constructed using bundles of 'tubes'. Though not a beautiful building, it was still the world's highest for 20 years!

Architects worldwide build high to prove their status and technology.

1933 Frank Lloyd Wright plans a 'half-mile-high' building to hold all Chicago's World Fair.

1947 The 39-storey U.N. Secretariat Building is built in New York on a site donated by J.D. Rockefeller Jr.

1966 Oscar Niemeyer's National Congress Building in Brasilia is one of his many designs in Brazil's modern capital.

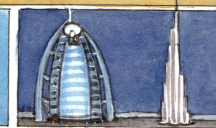

1970s Architects build Islamic-style skyscrapers in the Middle East.

Earthquakes and typhoons
Places like Japan and Taiwan have to deal with even more dangers when they build skyscrapers. The countries lie in typhoon and earthquake belts, and their modern buildings are specially strengthened to withstand the forces of nature.

Skyscraper Safety
After the terrible attacks on New York's World Trade Center's twin towers, architects and engineers have reassessed the safety of skyscrapers. The towers were built to be tin tubes with open floors. Experts believe the floor supports burnt due to the fire, causing each floor to collapse on to the one below. Engineers designing skyscrapers now include better fire proofing, a concrete core, and a plan to evacuate people very quickly.

Burj Dubai
(Dubai, Skidmore, Owings and Merrill)
Designed by New York architects, if it is built, this 800-metre-high (2,625 feet) skyscraper will streak ahead of the race, and became the world's highest skyscraper!

Freedom Tower
(a design to replace the World Trade Center, New York – Daniel Liebeskind)
Liebeskind won a bitterly-fought competition to fill the site of the World Trade Center. His tower will soar above a group of lower buildings, and it will be a significant 1,776 feet (541 metres) high, representing the year America declared its independence.

Taipei 101
(Taiwan, 2004, C.Y. Lee and C.P. Wang)
The finished 508 metre (1,667 feet), 101-storey building was planned to be the world's tallest and strongest skyscraper. Engineers say it can withstand the impact of a jumbo jet. Because of its height, the tower has very fast lifts, taking passengers to the top floor in just 39 seconds! C.Y. Lee designed it in Asian style, bamboo-like, dividing it into 8 sections. Eight is a Chinese lucky number and bamboo symbolises Taiwan's strong, fast-growing economy.

Petronas Tower,
(Kuala Lumpur, 1992-7, Cezar Pelli)
Malaysia's 452-metre-high (1,483 feet) twin pagoda towers were the world's highest building at the time, and were deliberately Asian in appearance.

Shanghai World Financial Centre
(Shanghai, 1997–2001, Kohn Pederson Fox)
This 492-metre-high (1,614 feet) tower, designed in 1997, is still one of the highest buildings in the world. The huge hole at its top is both beautiful and practical as it reduces wind resistance.

Terrorist attacks and natural disasters are risks for modern skyscrapers.

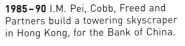

1979–86 Norman Foster's Hong Kong and Shanghai Bank is a tower on Hong Kong's skyline.

1985–90 I.M. Pei, Cobb, Freed and Partners build a towering skyscraper in Hong Kong, for the Bank of China.

1989–93 Jean Nouvel designs a cylindrical 'Tour Sans Fins' – a never-ending tower – for Paris.

1993–98 The 88-storey Jin Mao Tower in Shanghai is built according to Chinese feng shui ideas.

Robert Venturi (b. 1925)

POSTMODERN BUILDINGS
mid-1960s to today

A number of architects working in the mid-1960s grew tired of identical international city-centres – full of dull, slab-like, modern skyscrapers. They could see that interesting old communities were being torn down, only to be replaced with boring shopping malls and office blocks. One architect, Robert Venturi, decided to take action. He demanded complicated, messier, livelier and more enjoyable city architecture. This was part of a movement called Postmodernism. Postmodern skyscrapers were designed with a bottom, middle and a top, like Johnson's AT&T Building (1978–83), nicknamed 'the Chippendale Skyscraper' because the top looked like a piece of the famous furniture!

Teatro del Mondo
Aldo Rossi (1931–97)
(Venice, Italy, 1979)
Rossi began a fight-back against Italy's post-World War II political and architectural chaos. He did it by stressing extreme order, not with the messiness favoured by his fellow architects. The Teatro del Mondo, a temporary, colourful wooden theatre for the 1980 Venice Bienniale – afloat on a barge – was an example of this orderliness.

Public Services Building
Michael Graves (b. 1934)
(Portland, USA, 1980–2)
Resembling a stage design with its imaginative mixture of colours and materials, this cube-shaped building used ideas from the revolutionary 18th century French architect, Ledoux.

Vanna Venturi House
Robert Venturi, (b.1925)
(Philadelphia, USA, 1962)
Built for his mother, this house seemed like a typical American home with a porch – but it also re-worked ideas about proportion and architecture put forward by the 16th century architect Palladio, and Le Corbusier in the 20th century.

Piazza d'Italia
Charles Moore (1925–93)
(New Orleans, USA, 1975–80)
Moore was interested in architectural history and in creating a 'sense of place'. This piazza – or square – had an Italian-American sense of place in its eccentric use of colour, Classical Roman ideas, water, statues – and even a 3D map of Italy!

Neue Staatsgalerie & new chamber theatre
James Stirling (1926–92) & Michael Wilford (b. 1938)
(Stuttgart, Germany, 1977–84)
This German gallery was a clever mix of Classical ideas and colourful Postmodern design. In a difficult city site next to an older gallery, Stirling combined the old and the new in a fresh and interesting way, using historical details and modern technology.

Postmodern architects wanted to make cities interesting places to live.

1965–74 Charles Moore builds a bright and lively dormitory complex for Kresge College in Santa Cruz, California.

1970s Robert Stern works on a storefront for Best Products Inc. in Maryland, USA, using ancient Classical orders.

1976–78 SITE (Sculpture in the Environment) design an amusing building – the Tilt Showroom of Best Products Inc.

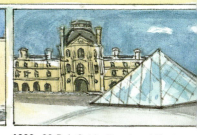

1983–89 Pei, Cobb, Freed and Partners use a glass pyramid design for the entrance to the Louvre Museum in Paris.

Frank Gehry (b. 1929)

CONTEMPORARY AND BEYOND

Renzo Piano (b. 1937)

Today half the world's population live in cities. In future, architects will have to use their skills to build smart, efficiently engineered buildings. At the same time, most architects will want to make their buildings eco-friendly, connecting them to the natural world. Some architects might recycle old buildings, giving them a new life instead of demolishing them.

Most cities grow in an unplanned way – invaded both by cars and international-style buildings like skyscrapers and stadiums. If wealthy people move to the suburbs, city centres can become derelict and unpleasant. But with careful planning, modern cities, like Barcelona, can be really enjoyable places to live. Future cities must follow their example.

Bankside Power Station, London (c. 2000) Originally by Giles Gilbert Scott, reworked by Swiss architects Herzog (b. 1950) and De Meuron (b. 1950) into today's **Tate Modern** gallery.

From the 1960s to the present day, industrial development has destroyed many fine old buildings, only to replace them with much poorer ones. A few architects have fought against this waste, reusing the best old buildings and combining old and new in one space.

Ecological Building (2004), Emilio Ambasz. Ecological Architecture is a way of creating sustainable communities that work in harmony with the Earth's biosphere, not against it. So, an eco-tower or pyramid must be heated by the sun, cooled by evaporation and use power and water extremely efficiently. In such a 'living' building, waste must be recycled, and rain must be collected for plants and also recycled for drinking. Buildings now on the drawing board intend to make the natural and built environment blend together to leave little impact on local ecology.

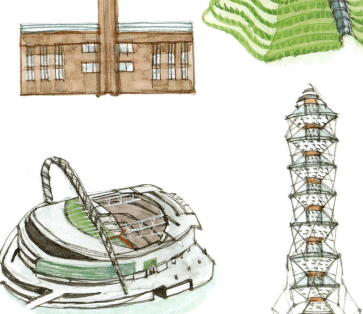

Co-Existence Research Project, New York and London (1985)
This optimistic Future Systems project was very influential in its day. It demonstrated a new way of creating a tower for mixed uses (eg offices, residential and leisure) – a Mother Structure of self-contained communities in the sky. Space Age research has brought about modular structures. They are repeatable and very adaptable – perfect for self-contained communities like space stations, moon bases, giant orbiting 'mother-structures' – or towers here on Earth.

Wembley Stadium (2007)
Begun in 2002 by the World Stadium team of architects, the finished National Stadium will hold over 90,000 spectators comfortably in steep tiers of seats, all with unobstructed views. The landmark Wembley arch, 133 metres high (436 feet), will support Wembley's sliding roof.

Future architects must make cities good places to live in.

1991–97 Frank O'Gehry's unusual Guggenheim museum in Bilbao, Spain, looks like a sculpture.

1998 Renzo Piano finishes his Jean-Marie Tjibaou Cultural Centre using natural curved structures made of steel, glass and timber.

1998 Nicholas Grimshaw designs giant linked bio-dome greenhouses in Cornwall's quarries, to house diverse plants in the 'Eden Project'.

1998 onwards Work continues on the International Space Station, as it orbits 131 kilometres (210 miles) above the Earth.

Glossary

Abdication   when a monarch gives up his or her throne.
Akropolis   a high fortified part of an ancient Greek city such as Athens. It is also sometimes spelled Acropolis.
Ambulatory   an aisle for walking along, usually in a church or monastery.
Amphitheatre   usually an unroofed circular building or stadium, for contests and spectacles, where tiers of seats surround a central space called an arena.
Anatomy   the study or science of the inside structure of a plant or animal.
Aqueduct   a man-made channel, usually on a bridge, for carrying water across a valley.
Arcade   a series of arches held up on piers (large, square vertical supports) or columns.
Architect   a designer of buildings who prepares plans and supervises construction.
Art Deco   a decorative, geometrical style, fashionable in the 1920s and 30s, which relied on fine workmanship and materials. The style was used in architecture, furniture and jewellery design.
Art Nouveau   an artistic and architectural style at the turn of the late 19th and early 20th centuries, characterised by the flowing, organic lines of stylised plants and animals.
Asia Minor   a peninsular in the westernmost part of Asia, taking in most of Turkey, and bounded by the Black, Aegean and Mediterranean seas.
Auditorium   the part of a theatre where the audience sits.

Balustrade   a railing supported by 'balusters' - ornamental short pillars.
Basilica   originally a large rectangular public building in ancient Rome, with a central nave and side aisle. It is also a long Christian church with a similar form.
Bio-Dome   a modern, man-made dome structure, most often built to hold diverse communities of plants.
Biosphere   the parts of the Earth's crust and atmosphere where living organisms live.
Boulevard   a broad tree-lined street or road.
Box Girder   a type of bridge construction that uses a hollow girder and has a square cross-section.
Britannia   a helmeted woman, holding a shield and trident, who from Roman times became the personification of Britain.
Buttress   a structure that gives support to the outside of a building. A flying buttress is a supporting arch through two floors connected to the upper part of the building or roof.
Byzantine   the area that was the eastern part of the Roman Empire, after it was divided in AD 395. Its capital became Byzantium, now Istanbul.

Cantilever   a long bracket or beam fixed at one end (like on a vertical pier on a bridge), which projects from a structure.
Classical   usually relating to the art, literature, culture, or architecture of Ancient Greece or Rome.
Coke   what is left of coal after the gasses have been removed. It is used in blast furnaces to produce molten iron.
Colonnades   a row of columns, often supporting a roof in Classical architecture.

Commission   a group of people entrusted to perform certain tasks or duties.
Cupola   a rounded dome.
Eco-Friendly   not harmful to the natural environment.

Façade   the main outside face of a building, usually at the front.
Follies   costly ornamental buildings that have no practical use.
Fresco   a watercolour painting made on a wall or ceiling while the plaster is still wet.
Frieze   a horizontal band, often decorated with sculpture or painting, and found in Classical architecture.
Functional   in architecture, buildings designed to be practical rather than decorative or attractive.

Geodesic Dome   a dome made from short struts, and constructed in a semi-circle shape.
Geometry   a branch of mathematics that deals with points, lines, surfaces and solids, and how they relate to one another.
Gothic   a style of architecture popular in Europe from the 12th century and characterised by pointed windows, rose windows, rib-vaulting and flying buttresses.
Greek Muses   in Greek mythology, the nine goddesses, daughters of Zeus, who inspired the arts and sciences.
Guild   a group of people who associate to help each other, or share a common goal, often medieval craftsmen.

Ice Age   a geological period when glacial ice spread over large areas of the Northern Hemisphere, beginning c. 2 million years ago and ending c. 12,000 years ago.
Imperial   magnificent and majestic, having the characteristics of an emperor or an empire.
Industrial Revolution   (c. 1750-1850) the change from an agricultural to an industrial economy. Britain pioneered this in the mid-18th century, with new inventions in steam power leading to textile factories, steam railways and rapidly increasing wealth from manufacturing.

Labyrinth   a network of passages, like a maze. It was originally where the mythical half-man, half-bull Minotaur lived in ancient Crete.
Lintel   the horizontal supporting piece (usually stone or wood) across the top of a door or window, or other vertical structure.
Load-Bearing   a structure such as a wall which carries the weight of the building so is vital to the building's safety and stability.

Machicolations   a defensive construction projecting out from the top of a medieval building or tower. Hot liquids and missiles can be hurled from openings in the floor.
Mason   a builder who works with stone.
Mass-Production   the making of a standard item in very large quantities using a mechanised factory process.
Mastaba   a simple bench-like ancient Egyptian tomb, with a flat roof and sloping sides, and a passageway leading to an underground tomb.

Medieval   the Middle Ages of Europe, between ancient and modern times, approximately between the 5th and 15th centuries.

Mesoamerica   the thin strip of land and countries between the large South and North American continents. It is also called Central America.

Minaret   a thin turret or tower at a mosque, from which men called muezzin call people to prayer at certain hours of the day.

Modernism   the modern fashion in art and architecture, which began in the 20th century.

Mosaic   small coloured pieces of glass or stone, arranged to make a picture or pattern.

Nave   the long central space of a church, from the main western entrance to the area where the 'transept' arms cross it at right angles.

Obelisk   a tapering, four-sided stone pillar or monument.

Organic   in art and architecture, forms and styles derived from plant and animal shapes.

Pagan   someone not belonging to one of the main world religions.

Pagoda   a Hindu or Buddhist temple, often a many-tiered tower, often found in India, China and Japan.

Palm Houses   large greenhouses built in the 19th century from iron and glass, to house palm plants and trees.

Pavilion   a decorative building, often in a garden, or a building used for entertainments.

Pedestrian   related to walking, a place where only walkers, not motorists, are allowed.

Pediment   a triangular front of a Classical-style building, above the portico (entrance porch) of columns.

Perspective   a system of drawing, invented in early 15th century Italy, where real or imaginary lines give the illusion of distance and 3-dimensional depth on a 2-dimensional surface.

Pier   a large vertical support, usually rectangular in its cross-section, used in bridge construction.

Plinth   in architecture, the square slab under a column, or the base which supports a statue.

Postmodernism   a late 20th-century name for designs which rejected Modernism's pure forms and techniques. Postmodern architects used a mixture of past styles, and also used ornament, colour and sculpture - sometimes humorously.

Prefabricate   to make sections (eg of a building) at one location, before assembling them at the finished site.

Prototype   an original thing which is the model from which copies or improvements are made.

Reformation   the religious movement of the 16th century which broke away from the Catholic Church and led to the establishment of the Protestant Church.

Renaissance   a renewed interest in art, architecture, literature and Thought which happened in Europe in the 14th to 16th centuries, using Classical Greek and Roman ideas.

Rib-vaulting   a curved stone or timber structure which supports a roof. Fan-vaulting is a variation of rib-vaulting.

Rivet   one of a series of nails or bolts that hold metal plates together.

Romanesque   a European style of architecture from the 11th and 12th centuries characterised by heavy walls and arches, and a basilica shape.

Sanctuary Roof   the roof of the sanctuary and the holiest place in a temple.

Sarcophagus   a stone coffin.

Sculpture   the art of making 3-dimensional forms by carving, chiselling or casting stone, clay or wood.

Serf   a labourer not allowed to leave the land on which he works.

Settlement   the colonisation of an area, or the actual place that people have settled.

Shrine   a place, such as a chapel or altar, which is sacred.

Slave   someone who is the legal property of another person.

Smelting   the extraction of metal from rock or ore by melting it at high temperatures.

Stone Age   a prehistoric period when weapons and tools were made from stone.

Storey   all the rooms in a building that are on one floor. There may be several storeys to the building.

Sumerian   someone living in Sumer, an ancient civilisation and a district of Babylon, in Mesopotamia.

Surveyor   a person who views a building's condition and measures land.

Suspension Cable   thick wires hanging from tall pier structures on a bridge, which support the suspended roadway.

Symmetry   a structure that, even after being divided, has parts of equal shape and size. A symmetrical structure usually appears to be very well balanced.

Tetanus   a potentially fatal bacterial disease that makes muscles rigid and likely to suffer spasms. It is sometimes called 'lockjaw'.

Tomb   a large underground vault or space where the dead are buried.

Transept   the arms of a cross-shaped church, built at right angles to the long nave.

Urban Revolution   an historical time beginning thousands of years ago when people began to leave farming for the city to specialise in other skills. They built towns and created more complex class and social systems.

Vault   an underground chamber, or a continuous arch or series of arches, built in brick or stone.

Ventilation   the free circulation of fresh air into and out of a room.

Vista   a long, narrow view, sometimes between rows of trees or buildings.

Whitewash   a mixture of ground chalk and quicklime, which is used to whiten walls and ceilings.

Ziggurat   a rectangular, stepped tower topped with a temple, usually found in Mesopotamia.

Index